Our Earth
and the
Solar System

Ken Graun

Introduction by **Thomas J. Bopp**

Cover Design by **Debra K. Niwa**

Ken Press

To all the children of the world, never stop striving.
K. G.

The beautiful heavens above are full of mysteries and unanswered questions.
Perhaps you can be someone who will find some of the answers.
T. J. B.

For Jesse.
D. K. N.

Publisher's Cataloging-in-Publication

Graun, Ken.
 Our Earth and the solar system / Ken Graun;
introduction by Thomas J. Bopp; cover design by Debra K. Niwa. — 1st ed.
 p. cm. — (21st century astronomy series)
 LCCN: 99-068976
 ISBN: 1-928771-02-5
 SUMMARY: Provides facts about the sun, planets, and comets in our solar system.

 1. Solar system — Juvenile literature. 2. Astronomy—Juvenile literature. I. Title

 QB501.3.G73 2001   523.2
                           QBI00-860

Published by Ken Press, Tucson, Arizona, United States of America ★ www.kenpress.com
Printed in Hong Kong by South Sea Pacific Press
1 3 5 7 9 10 8 6 4 2

Introduction &
Table of Contents

Top, from left:
Thomas Bopp,
Ken Graun,
Skylar St. Charles,
Debra Niwa,
Jesse Niwa,
Brandon Williams
and
Mason Madea.
Bottom, from left:
Ryan Lindsey,
Delaney Gould,
Sean Lindsey
and
Adrea Graun.

Hi, my name is Thomas Bopp. In 1995, I discovered one of the largest and brightest comets ever witnessed in the history of mankind. When a comet graces our skies, everyone in the world can look up, see its splendor and share in something that is wonderful.

Sharing is what this book is about. It shares with you the grandeur and beauty of our solar system. This is the ideal starting place to learn about astronomy. Astronomy has always been my favorite science, but all of the sciences are important. The knowledge we have gained from the sciences has allowed us to create the most technologically advanced society ever.

I want to encourage every one of you to work hard in school. Do your best and learn as much as possible. This is important because you are the future. Now, go out and discover something that will make this world an even better place to live in!

Our Solar System

A solar system is a star that has planets, asteroids and comets revolving about it. Stars are at the center of every solar system because they are so large that their gravity keeps all the other objects bound to them.

Solar systems form inside huge hydrogen clouds, called nebulae. A solar system starts as a protoplanetary disk, which is a concentration of hydrogen gas, other elements, rocks and ice particles. A protoplanetary disk can take a million or more years to condense into the star, planets, asteroids and comets that make up a solar system.

Our Earth is part of a solar system. We call the star that we orbit "the Sun" or "Sol." Our solar system has nine planets and billions of asteroids and comets. Its diameter to Pluto is over seven billion miles.

Astronomers are discovering planets around other stars, but they have not yet found a planet like Earth.

This sentence will help you remember the order of the planets from the Sun. My Very Energetic Mother Just Served Us Nine Pizzas.

Our Solar System

Age: about 4.5 billion years

Diameter: 7,350,000,000 miles or 11 light hours

The nine planets in order from the Sun are: Mercury, Venus, Earth, Mars, Jupiter, Saturn, Uranus, Neptune and Pluto. The *asteroid belt* is between Mars and Jupiter.

Comets: The majority of comets reside far out in a giant cloud called the Oort cloud, which surrounds the rest of the solar system. This cloud of comets extends halfway to our nearest solar neighbor, the star Proxima Centauri, which is 4.2 light years away.

Solar systems form within giant
hydrogen clouds called nebulae, like the
Eagle nebula pictured here, located in
the constellation Serpens. This nebula is
so large that many solar systems are
forming inside at the same time.

This is what the Sun looks like through a special solar filter called a hydrogen-alpha filter. This filter allows you to see prominences and the Sun's mottled surface.

The corona is a veil of very hot hydrogen gas that surrounds the Sun. It can be seen with the naked eye during a total solar eclipse, which happens when the Moon passes in front of the Sun.

Hot spots like this are many thousands of degrees hotter than the normal surface temperature.

This little blue ball shows the size of the Earth compared to the Sun pictured here.

A *Prominence* is an eruption on the Sun that shoots outward and often loops back to the surface.

Sun Facts

Diameter: 865,000 miles

Surface temperature: 10,000° F

Sunspot temperature: 6,300° F

Temperature at core: 27,000,000° F

Composition: 92% hydrogen gas, 8% helium gas plus traces of many other elements

Source of energy: Nuclear fusion — the energy released when four hydrogen atoms are forced together to form one helium atom in the core.

The Sun

Our Sun is a star just like the other stars in the night sky. However, our Sun is special to us because it is the star that our Earth revolves around.

The nature of stars

What is a star? A huge ball of hydrogen gas that creates energy by a special process called nuclear fusion. Since stars are very large, the pressure at their centers is so great that hydrogen atoms are forced together to become helium atoms. During this "fusing" process, a very small amount of matter gets converted into an enormous amount of energy. We see this energy as the brilliant light of the Sun.

Although our Sun is huge, it is only an average-sized star. The largest stars are gigantic. Betelgeuse, in the constellation Orion, has a diameter 400 times greater than our Sun. Small stars are about a third the size of our Sun. Our Sun is yellowish in color. Stars with cooler surface temperatures have a reddish color, while those that are hotter look blue or white.

A star like our Sun will shine for 10 to 12 billion years. The largest stars will last less than 10 million years, whereas smaller stars may last for a trillion years or more.

The Sun's surface

When you glance at the Sun, the bright part that you see is called the photosphere. Photo means light, so you are seeing the part of the Sun that gives off visible light. If you attached a solar filter to a telescope, you would be able to see sunspots

This is what the Sun looks like through a regular "white light" solar filter. Sunspots can be seen on its yellowish surface, called the photosphere.

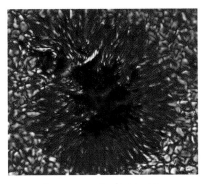

A sunspot close up. The darker, inner part is called the umbra, and the lighter surrounding area is called the penumbra. Sunspots are about 4,000 F° cooler than the Sun's normal surface temperature of 10,000° F.

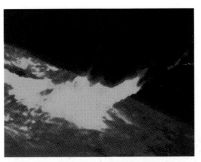

Flares shoot out positively or negatively charged particles, called ions, into the solar system. These particles often interact with our atmosphere to produce the Northern and Southern Lights.

on the photosphere. These dark spots grow and then dissolve away. Many are larger than the Earth. Sunspots indicate areas of intense magnetic fields.

The Sun's atmosphere

Immediately above the photosphere is a thin red layer of gas, about 1,000 miles thick, called the chromosphere. This layer separates the lower photosphere from the outer corona. The corona is a magnificent veil of hydrogen gas reaching millions of degrees in temperature and extending for millions of miles from the Sun. The corona is visible as an irregular halo surrounding the Sun during a total solar eclipse.

Cycles of activity

Our Sun becomes very active about every 11 years. During this time, the number of sunspots, prominences and flares increases. Over 100 sunspots per day can often be counted. Huge prominences jet off from the surface and often loop back. And, flares shoot out charged particles into the solar system that create the wonderful displays of the northern Aurora Borealis and the southern Aurora Australis on Earth.

WARNING
We all glance at the Sun but you should *NEVER* stare at it because it will damage your eyes. And, *NEVER* look directly at the Sun through binoculars, a telescope or camera because you will be instantly and permanently blinded. You need special filters to safely view the Sun through these optical instruments.

Mercury

All of the planets were named after ancient Roman and Greek mythological gods. Mercury, the closest planet to the Sun, was named after a Roman god who had wings attached to his feet and a helmet on his head. He swiftly delivered messages to the other gods. As the name so well implies, the planet Mercury revolves rapidly around the Sun, more swiftly than any of the other planets.

The Terrestrial planets

Mercury is known as a terrestrial planet because it is Earth-like, that is, it is composed of rock-type materials and has a solid surface that you can stand and walk on. The four terrestrial planets are Mercury, Venus, Earth and Mars.

Just like our Moon

Mercury resembles our Moon. Just like our Moon, it is pitted with craters and has no atmosphere. And, Mercury is just slightly larger than our Moon.

Surface and interior

The craters on Mercury were formed from a heavy bombardment of asteroids and comets during the first billion years of the solar system's existence. The interior of Mercury, once molten, has cooled and is now solid. It is composed mostly of iron ore.

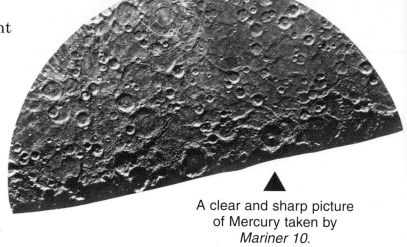

A clear and sharp picture of Mercury taken by *Mariner 10.*

This is the size of the Sun as it would appear from Mercury.

How big would the Sun appear from each of the other planets in our solar system?

Look for the yellow Suns on the following pages and compare their sizes for yourself.

So close to the Sun

Mercury is very difficult to study with a telescope because it is so close to the Sun. All of the detailed pictures of this planet were obtained by the *Mariner 10* spacecraft in 1975. *Mariner 10* photographed less than half of Mercury's surface.

Phases like our Moon

Since Mercury orbits inside of Earth's orbit, we can see it cycle through phases, just like our Moon. When we see phases, we are viewing the day and night side of a planet or moon at the same time.

Mercury in the sky

Mercury can be seen as a fairly bright star but most people miss this planet because it rises just a little before sunrise or sets shortly after sunset.

Mercury is disappointing to view through a telescope because it is always low in the sky where atmospheric turbulence is the greatest. In a telescope, Mercury appears as a bright, bubbling, color-changing blob of light. The bubbling makes it difficult to even see its phases.

A false-color picture of Mercury. It is called false-color because the colors are not the actual colors on Mercury's surface. False coloring is often used by scientists to make features stand out. The colors in this picture indicate the different types of materials that make up Mercury's surface. Colors that are the same indicate the same type of surface material. There are many false-color pictures in this book.

In 1975, the Mariner 10 spacecraft sent back images of Mercury. It is the only spacecraft that has visited this planet.

Mercury Facts

Diameter: 3,032 miles

Distance from the Sun: 36,000,000 miles

Atmosphere: Mercury has no atmosphere — no air!

Temperatures: 800° F on day side, −300° F on night side

Rotation on Axis (Mercury's day): 59 days

Revolution about Sun (Mercury's Year): 88 days

Moons: Mercury has no moons

Mercury's surface is pitted with craters just like the Earth's Moon.

Only 45% of Mercury's surface was imaged by *Mariner 10*.

The *Pioneer Venus Orbiter* circled Venus from 1978 to 1992 and gathered general information about the planet. In 1992, it ran out of fuel and burned up in Venus' atmosphere.

This is a false-color mapping produced by using radar imagery from the spacecraft *Magellan* in the early 1990s. Blue indicates low areas while red indicates the higher areas. Areas with the same color are at the same altitude. Venus' surface can only be mapped with radar because its clouds are too thick to see through.

Try This

1. Look at Venus through binoculars or a small telescope when it appears brightest. Can you make out a crescent shape?

2. Go outside and find a dark area without lights when Venus is bright and the Moon is not out. Instead of looking up, look down on the ground for the shadows that Venus casts.

NEED HELP? VISIT OUR WEBSITE LISTED ON PAGE 36 FOR INFORMATION ON FINDING AND OBSERVING VENUS.

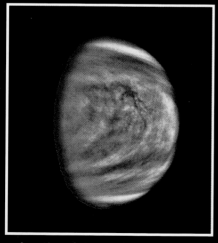

Another false-color picture of Venus. This one highlights the swirls in its clouds. Venus' clouds are solid white to the eye.

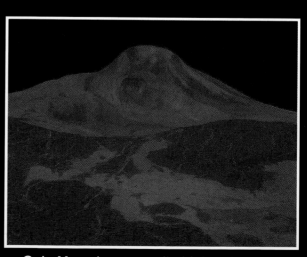

Gula Mons is a two mile high volcano on Venus' surface. The coloring is based on images from the *Venera 13* and *14* spacecraft that landed on Venus in the early 1980s.

Venus

Venus was named after the Roman goddess of love. It is the planet that is closest to Earth and the only planet similar in size to Earth. Before spacecraft visited Venus, it was considered Earth's sister planet. Read on and discover how different Venus really is from Earth.

Earth-like or not?

Venus is a terrestrial planet that is composed of rock-type material. Like Earth, it has a surface that you can stand and walk on.

Venus' atmosphere consists mainly of the colorless gas carbon dioxide. In chemistry, carbon dioxide is written as CO_2. The "C" stands for one atom of carbon that is bonded to two atoms of oxygen (the "O").

Venus is also completely covered with clouds that are so thick, it is impossible to see through them. No one knew what was beneath these white, opaque clouds until exploratory spacecraft visited the planet in the late 1970s. What they found took scientists by surprise. Venus is an inferno!

Sulfuric acid clouds

The whiteness in Venus' atmosphere is from clouds of sulfuric acid. The surface of Venus has numerous volcanos that continually release sulfur dioxide which combines with a small amount of water vapor in the atmosphere to form sulfuric acid, a very strong acid.

Greenhouse effect

What happens inside a car that is out in the Sun with its windows rolled up? The inside heats up because the windows trap the heat from the sunlight.

The same thing happens to Venus. Its atmosphere of carbon dioxide acts like the windows of a car, trapping the sunlight and heating the atmosphere. This type of heating is called the greenhouse effect. On Venus, the greenhouse effect keeps the temperature near the surface at 900° F, the hottest of any planet. This is hot enough to melt the metal lead.

Pressure cooker

Overall, Venus' atmosphere contains about 100 times more gas than Earth's. This "heavy" atmosphere produces tremendous pressure, over 90 times greater than on Earth. The same pressure can be found at 3,000 feet below the ocean's surface.

The surface

Venus is a barren planet that is riddled with rocks, volcanos and some craters. Scientists believe that its surface may circulate with its upper interior and thus renew itself every 100 million years.

Upside down, backwards and a long day

Venus rotates nearly upside down compared to the other planets. As a result, if you viewed Venus from the top of the solar system (from the direction of Earth's north pole), it would appear to rotate backward. Also, Venus rotates very slowly on its axis. It takes longer to rotate once on its axis than to revolve around the Sun.

The brightest planet

Often, Venus is the brightest "star" in the sky. Its white clouds make it highly reflective and its closeness to Earth makes it even brighter. Venus does cast shadows if the Moon is not out.

The size of the Sun from Venus. Compare it to the others.

Venus Facts

Diameter: 7,520 miles

Distance from the Sun: 67,200,000 miles

Atmosphere: 96% carbon dioxide gas, 4% nitrogen gas plus traces of other gases

Temperature: averages 900° F which is hot enough to melt the metal lead

Rotation on Axis (Venus' Day): 243 days — longer than its year!

Revolution about Sun (Venus' Year): 225 days

Moons: Venus has no moons

A view of Earth from the *Galileo Orbiter* spacecraft on its way to Jupiter in 1990.

This satellite, *LAGEOS I*, orbits Earth and is used, with laser beams, to measure the movement of the Earth's surface.

The Earth is our home. And, as far as astronomers know, the only planet with life. No one understands exactly how life developed on Earth but we are certain that two major factors are necessary for life to start and then to flourish. First, a planet must have liquid water. Our Earth's surface is 71% water. Second, the temperature must stay in a narrow range. If the Earth were just a little closer or a little farther away from the Sun than it is now, it would be either too hot or

The original seven American *Mercury* astronauts.
Top, from left: Alan Shepard (first American in space), Virgil "Gus" Grissom and L. Gordon Cooper.
Bottom, from left: Walter Schirra, Donald "Deke" Slayton, John Glenn (first American to orbit the Earth) and Scott Carpenter.

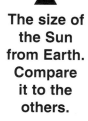

Recovery of the *Mercury-Atlas 4* orbital spacecraft in 1961. All of the early American spacecraft splash-landed in the oceans.

Earth Facts

Diameter: 7,910 miles

Distance from the Sun: 93,000,000 miles

Atmosphere: 77% nitrogen, 21% oxygen, 1% water vapor, 1% argon plus traces of many other gases

Temperatures: averages 59° F, highest temperature 136° F, lowest temperature −129° F

Rotation on axis (Earth's Day): 24 hours

Revolution about Sun (Earth's Year): 365 days, 8 hours

Thickness of atmosphere: Our atmosphere extends for hundreds of miles, but most of it lies within 55 miles of the surface.

The size of the Sun from Earth. Compare it to the others.

The Earth

cold for life to flourish. There are many other factors necessary for life to flourish, but if these two conditions were not met, humans, animals and plants would not exist.

Earth Timeline

4.5 billion year ago • Earth is formed
3.5 billion years ago • simple life appears
245 to 65 million years ago • dinosaurs roam
Over 2 million years ago • human ancestors make stone tools
100,000 years ago • humans spread across the globe
10,000 years ago • pyramid building begins in Egypt
753 BC to 450 AD • Roman Empire
855 AD • Chinese invent gunpowder
500 to 1500 AD • castles built throughout Europe
1550 • modern science begins
1608 • telescope invented and used to explore sky
1804 • first steam locomotive
1887 • first automobiles
1903 • first successful airplane flight
1914 • first experimental rockets
1961 • Yuri Gagarin becomes first person in space
1969 • Neil Armstrong becomes first person to walk on Moon
1976 • *Voyager 1 & 2* launched to explore outer planets
1983 • first Space Shuttle flight

1987 • first planets discovered around other stars
1990 • *Hubble Space Telescope* placed into orbit
1994 • Comet Shoemaker-Levy 9 crashes into Jupiter
1995 • Comet Hale-Bopp discovered
1997 • first roving vehicle explores Mars
1998 • beginning of *International Space Station*
2000 • first indications that liquid water may lie beneath the surface of Mars

An artist's picture of what the *International Space Station* may look like when completed, which should be sometime in the early years of the 21st century. This space station is being built through the cooperation of 16 countries.

A. Blast-off of the space shuttle *Discovery* in 1998 with John Glenn aboard.

B. An illustration of the shuttle, above the Earth, with cargo bay doors open.

C. A fisheye view of the inside of *Discovery's* flight deck (the cockpit).

Moon Facts

Diameter: 2,160 miles

Distance from the Earth: 240,000 miles

Atmosphere: The moon has no atmosphere — no air!

Temperatures: 214° F in sunlight to −300° F on the night side

Rotation on Axis: 27 days, 12 hours

Revolution about Earth: 27 days, 12 hours

One crew member aboard the Command and Service Modules orbited the Moon while the other two explored the Moon's surface. The Command Module is the cone-shaped nose.

Six Apollo missions landed 12 men on the Moon between 1969 and 1972. Their journeys began by blasting off from Cape Canaveral atop a Saturn V (5) rocket. These missions ended when the Command Modules splashed into an ocean with three astronauts aboard.

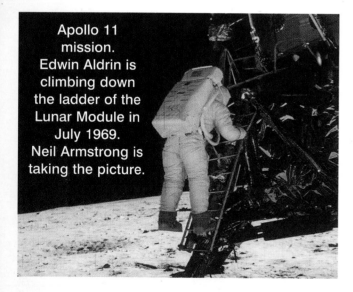

Apollo 11 mission. Edwin Aldrin is climbing down the ladder of the Lunar Module in July 1969. Neil Armstrong is taking the picture.

Try This

1. Look at the Moon through binoculars or a telescope. You will be able to see many craters and plains. The craters appear their sharpest when they are near the terminator, which is the line that separates the lighted side from the dark side.

2. Look at the Moon through binoculars when it is full and see if you can spot impact rays coming from the crater named Tycho.

The same side of the Moon always faces Earth. At one time, the Moon rotated, but gravity energy exchanged between the Earth and Moon has caused one side to face us.

The Earth's Moon

The Moon is visible during the day and, of course, we see it at night. It is forever cycling through phases, from a crescent to full and back. The phases occur as the Moon circles the Earth and are nothing more than our seeing the day and night side at the same time.

Man on the Moon

On July 20, 1969, Neil Armstrong became the first person to walk on the Moon. The last astronauts to visit were Eugene Cernan and Harrison Schmitt in December 1972. Schmitt, a geologist, was the first scientist in space and the only scientist to walk on the Moon.

Impacts galore

The Moon is full of craters. They vary in size and reach over 100 miles in diameter. Most of these bowl shaped depressions were formed when meteoroids, asteroids and comets impacted the surface over four billion years ago. The darker, smooth areas on the Moon are called maria or plains. These plains were formed when very large asteroids or comets struck deep into the Moon, releasing interior lava that flowed to the surface. Scientists believe that the interior of the Moon has completely cooled and is no longer molten.

First lunar landing, Apollo 11 mission, July 20, 1969, commanded by Neil Armstrong.

The creation of the Moon

The Moon was formed when an object as large as Mars slammed into the Earth over four billion years ago. How do we know this? The men who went to the Moon brought back rocks that contain the same rock-type materials found in the Earth's crust.

The man-in-the-Moon

Can you see the man-in-the-Moon? When people look at the full Moon, they try to see different things for fun. What do you see?

If you were on the Moon, you would quickly notice that the Earth would not move in the sky. It would not rise or set, but simply hover in one place and cycle through phases like the Moon does from Earth! ▶

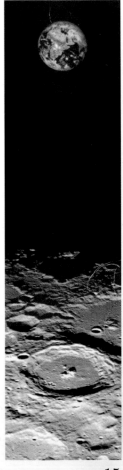

Mars Facts

Diameter: 4,200 miles

Distance from the Sun: 142,000,000 miles

Atmosphere: 95% carbon dioxide, 3% nitrogen, 1.6% argon, 0.2% oxygen

Temperatures: averages −81° F with a high of 72° F and a low of −274° F

Rotation on Axis (Mars' Day): 24 hours, 37 minutes

Revolution about Sun (Mars' Year): 687 days

Moons: Mars has two small moons named Phobos and Deimos

A picture of Mars taken in 1998 by the *Mars Global Surveyor*, which orbits 1,690 miles above the red planet. The long scar is actually a 2,500 mile long canyon called Valles Marineris.

The size of the Sun from Mars. Compare it to the others.

The moons of Mars. Phobos, in front, is 17 miles in length and orbits Mars in 7 hours, 42 minutes at a distance of 5,830 miles. Deimos is 10 miles long and orbits Mars in 1 day, 7 hours at a distance of 14,600 miles.

Olympus Mons is the largest inactive volcano in the solar system. The center depression is 56 miles wide and the total area of the volcano is the same as the state of Arizona.

Mars

Mars is named after the Roman god of war because of its red color. However, when we think of Mars, we often think of Martians. This idea started in the late 1800s when Giovanni Schiaparelli of Italy and Percival Lowell of America made drawings of what they thought to be canals. Lowell believed that the canals were built by Martians to transport water from the poles to the lower latitudes. Mars does not have canals or Martians but these ideas ignited imaginations throughout the world.

Surface and atmosphere

Since Mars' diameter is one-half of Earth's, its total surface area turns out to be about the same as the total land area on Earth. As you can see from the pictures on these pages, the surface of Mars resembles rocky desert.

Except for Earth, Mars is the most habitable planet in our solar system. However, you would need a light space suit to walk around on Mars. Its atmosphere is very thin, only 1/100 that of Earth's and even though its atmosphere is not poisonous, you could not breath it to stay alive.

Water

Mars has frozen water at its north pole and liquid water underground. Water is absolutely necessary for humans to survive an extended stay on another planet.

Captured asteroids

The two moons of Mars are believed to be captured asteroids because their irregular shapes and composition are like other asteroids.

Observing Mars

About every two years, Mars gets close to Earth so that surface colors can be observed in small telescopes. At this time, Mars is also at its brightest and even outshines Jupiter. To see surface coloration, you need at least a 4-inch diameter telescope and must use magnifications from 150x to 400x.

A picture of the southern polar cap, taken during the summer by the *Viking 2* orbiting spacecraft in 1977. This cap spans about 250 miles and is composed of frozen carbon dioxide (dry ice).

A panoramic view of Mars from the *Mars Pathfinder* in 1997. Below, next to the rock is *Sojourner*, the first roving vehicle ever used to explore the surface of another planet.

One of the best pictures of Mars taken by the Earth orbiting *Hubble Space Telescope*. Compare the detail in this picture to the one from the *Mars Global Surveyor* on the opposite page.

The Asteroid Belt

The asteroid belt lies between Mars and Jupiter. It is composed of about a billion chunks of rock that vary in size from a few hundred feet to over 500 miles across.

None of the asteroids have an atmosphere. Most have odd shapes and resemble potatoes. The asteroids are pitted with many craters, formed from being struck by other asteroids. Their colors range from reddish and light brown to dark gray. Asteroids are made of the metals nickel and iron as well as various silicates; that is, sand, quartz and other rock-type materials.

The asteroids are remnants left over from the formation of the solar system. They are not material from a planet that never formed or a planet that exploded.

The asteroid belt is not crowded like it appears on this page and in many science fiction movies. Instead, the individual asteroids are very far apart from one another.

The size of the Sun from the Asteroid Belt. Compare this to the other planets.

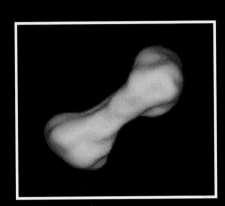

There are even asteroids shaped like dog bones. This asteroid, named Kleopatra, was imaged using radar instead of a camera. It is 135 miles long and 58 miles wide, which is about the size of New Jersey.

Asteroid Facts

Largest asteroids: Ceres, the largest asteroid, is roughly spherical and has a diameter of 568 miles. Pallas, the second largest, is more elongated and is 324 miles in length.

Distance from the Sun: the asteroid belt is wide with distances varying from 175,000,000 to 375,000,000 miles

Composition: they are made of metal ores and rock-type material

Revolution period about Sun: varies from 3 1/2 years to 6 1/2 years depending on distance

This asteroid, named Ida, is orbited by another very small asteroid called Dactyl. Ida is 32 miles in length and Dactyl is about one mile in diameter.

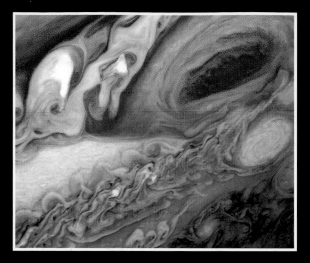

Jupiter's cloud belts are beautiful and complex. The Great Red Spot, which appears in both of these pictures, is a giant vortex, similar to a hurricane. The colors in the left picture are enhanced while the picture above uses false colors to bring out details in the clouds.

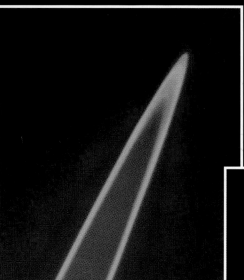

The spacecraft *Galileo*, launched in 1989, arrived and was placed into orbit around Jupiter in late 1995. It has provided us with incredible views of the four Galilean moons.

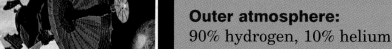

The size of the Sun from Jupiter. Compare it to the others.

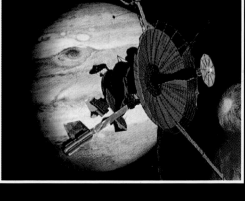

▲ Jupiter has a very faint and simple ring system which is not visible to telescopes on Earth.

Both Io and Europa experience huge gravitational forces from Jupiter, called tidal forces, that pull and tug on these moons.

Right. A volcano erupting on Io.

Far right. Europa is covered with a layer of solid ice. Liquid water may lie underneath.

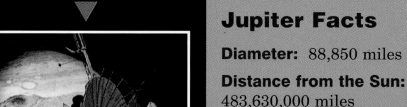

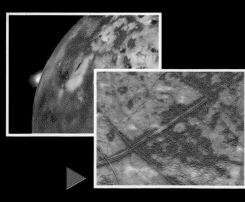

Jupiter Facts

Diameter: 88,850 miles

Distance from the Sun: 483,630,000 miles

Outer atmosphere: 90% hydrogen, 10% helium

Interior: Liquid metallic hydrogen

Temperature just below cloudtops: $-243°$ F

Rotation on Axis (Jupiter's Day): 9 hours, 50 minutes

Revolution about Sun (Jupiter's Year): 11 years, 314 days

Moons: Jupiter has 17 known moons, but only the 4 Galilean moons can be seen in small telescopes.

Jupiter

Jupiter is named after the supreme Roman god, ruler over all the other mythological gods. Jupiter was so named not because it was the largest planet but because it is consistently the brightest planet in the night sky. It is just a coincidence that Jupiter also turned out to be the largest planet in our solar system, because it was named thousands of years before anyone knew its size and what it really was.

The gas giants

Jupiter, Saturn, Uranus and Neptune are called gas giants because they are the four largest planets in our solar system and are composed mainly of hydrogen gas. The gas giants do not have surfaces that you can stand on, only atmospheres that extend inward for thousands of miles. The interiors of the gas giants are different from the terrestrial rock-type planets like Earth. Below their clouds lie a hot, soupy mixture of gases. And, in the case of Jupiter and Saturn, they also have an inner core of liquid metallic hydrogen which is hydrogen gas compressed so much, it takes on the properties of metal, including the ability to conduct electricity.

Jupiter's clouds and the Great Red Spot

Jupiter's atmosphere has countless bands of clouds. They are very complex and show a tremendous amount of variation. There are two very distinct bands, one in the northern hemisphere called the North Equatorial Belt and the other is in the southern hemisphere that is called the South Equatorial Belt. The most unique feature on Jupiter is its Great Red Spot. This giant vortex, similar to a hurricane, extends into the South Equatorial Belt. It has been observed for over 150 years. No one knows if it is a permanent feature but its color does change.

The Galilean moons

Jupiter has four large moons, called the Galilean moons, in honor of Galileo Galilei, who was one of the first scientists to observe them in 1610. Io, the closet of the four to Jupiter has very active volcanoes. Next out is Europa, which may have a vast ocean under its surface of ice. Ganymede, the largest of the four, is the largest moon in the solar system and is larger than Mercury and Pluto. Finally, there is Callisto which has craters with multi-rings around them.

The Four Galilean Moons

IO
Diameter: 2,255 miles
Distance from Jupiter: 262,000 miles
Revolution: 1 day, 18 hours

EUROPA
Diameter: 1,950 miles
Distance from Jupiter: 416,900 miles
Revolution: 3 days, 13 hours

GANYMEDE
Diameter: 3,270 miles
Distance from Jupiter: 664,900 miles
Revolution: 7 days, 4 hours

CALLISTO
Diameter: 2,980 miles
Distance from Jupiter: 1,171,000 miles
Revolution: 16 days, 17 hours

Try This

1. Look at Jupiter through binoculars. The bright "stars" next to it are the Galilean moons. How many can you see?

2. Observe Jupiter through a telescope using 50 to 100x magnification. You should be able to see the North and South Equatorial Belts and movement of the inner Galilean moons in as little as 15 minutes.

NEED HELP? VISIT OUR WEBSITE LISTED ON PAGE 36 FOR INFO ON OBSERVING JUPITER.

Saturn as it appeared when the *Voyager 2* spacecraft flew by in 1981. Can you see the three major rings in this picture? The outermost ring is called the A ring. It is separated from the bright B ring by the Cassini division. The A and B rings can be seen with a small telescope. The inner-most dark ring is called the C ring.

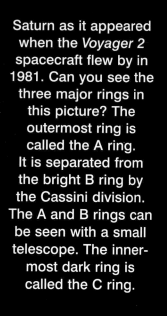

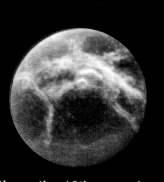

Dione, the 12th moon from Saturn, can be seen in a small telescope as a faint speck of light very near the planet. This moon is 700 miles in diameter and revolves around Saturn in less than three days.

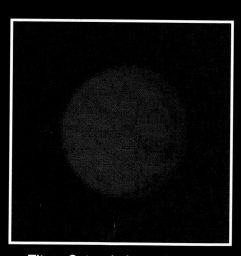

Titan, Saturn's largest moon, is the second largest moon in the solar system and has an atmosphere composed mostly of nitrogen gas.

The rings of Saturn are actually a series of narrow bands called ringlets. This false-color picture highlights the ringlets.

The size of the Sun from Saturn. Compare it to the others.

Saturn

When you think of a planet, which planet do you think of first? For most of us, Saturn comes to mind first because of its magnificent rings. Saturn was named after the Roman god of agriculture and is the second largest planet in our solar system.

Like Jupiter, Saturn is a gas giant. It does not have a surface that you could stand on. Its atmosphere is composed mostly of hydrogen gas but it does have some helium. Saturn's cloud belts are much simpler and less distinct than those on Jupiter.

The floating giant

Saturn is the only planet in our solar system that has a density less than 1. Density is a measure that compares the weight of equal volumes of material. Pure water has a density of exactly 1. Materials with densities of less than 1 float in water. So, Saturn would actually float if there were an ocean big enough to put it in.

The rings

Saturn is distinguished from all the other planets by its magnificent rings. The rings are actually a series of thousands of narrow rings called ringlets. Each ringlet is composed of billions of small rocks and ice chunks about an inch across. There are two bright groups of ringlets that are called the A and B rings. These two groups are visible in small telescopes and can also be seen in the picture on the facing page. Between them is a 2,900 mile gap called the Cassini division

Mimas, the 7th moon from Saturn, resembles the *Death Star* from the movie *Star Wars*™. The large dish crater is called Herschel and is 81 miles across. Mimas has a diameter of 242 miles, is 116,000 miles from Saturn, and revolves around the planet in less than a day.

that can sometimes be seen with a small telescope. The outer A ring has a diameter of 170,000 miles and the thickness of the rings varies from 30 to 100 feet.

Until 1977, astronomers thought Saturn was the only planet with rings, but we know today from Earth-based observations and images taken by exploring spacecraft that all four gas giants have them. Still, none are as visible or developed as Saturn's.

Saturn Facts

Diameter: 75,000 miles

Distance from the Sun: 887,000,000 miles

Outer atmosphere: 97% hydrogen, 3% helium

Interior: Liquid metallic hydrogen

Temperature near cloudtops: −301° F

Rotation on Axis (Saturn's Day): 10 hours, 14 minutes

Revolution about Sun (Saturn's Year): 29 years, 153 days

Moons: Saturn has 18 known moons. Titan, the largest, has a diameter of 3,200 miles.

Try This

Note: Saturn is twice as far away from the Earth as Jupiter and usually appears much smaller in a telescope than expected.

1. Observe Saturn through a telescope using 100 to 200x magnification. Now, take a closer look at the area right around the rings. Can you spot up to four faint specks that are Saturn's moons?

2. The rings of Saturn vary in how much they are slanted. Observe Saturn over the years and see how they change. In January of 2009, they will be "edge-on" and invisible from Earth.

NEED HELP? VISIT OUR WEBSITE LISTED ON PAGE 36 FOR INFO ON FINDING AND OBSERVING SATURN.

A sliver of Uranus. All of the planets and moons in our solar system cycle through phases. Seeing a phase is nothing more than viewing the day and night side of a planet or moon at the same time.

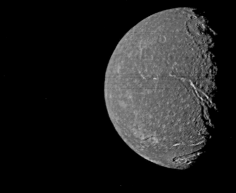

Titania, the largest moon of Uranus, has a diameter of exactly 1,000 miles.

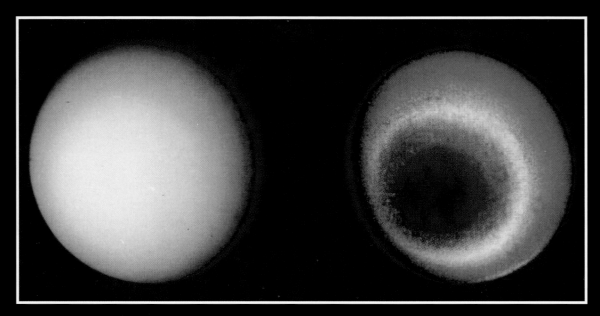

The picture on the left is how Uranus looks to the naked eye. On the right is a false-color picture that enhances the temperature differences in the atmosphere. Although Uranus' atmosphere appears plain and cloudless in these *Voyager 2* pictures, the *Hubble Space Telescope* has imaged clouds on this gas giant.

Uranus Facts

Diameter: 31,764 miles

Distance from the Sun: 1,784,000,000 miles

Outer atmosphere: 83% hydrogen, 15% helium, 2% methane

Inner core: possibly a small rock core surrounded by a soup of various "ices," which is actually a hot mixture of water, methane and ammonia

Temperature near cloudtops: −323° F

Rotation on Axis (Uranus' Day): 17 hours, 54 minutes

Revolution about Sun (Uranus' Year): 83 years, 274 days

Moons: Uranus has 21 known moons, the most of any planet. Titania, the largest, has a diameter of 1,000 miles and orbits Uranus in 8 days, 17 hours at a distance of 271,000 miles.

Uranus

Uranus (pronounced YOOR-uh-nus) was discovered by Sir William Herschel of England in 1781 while he was exploring the sky, recording nebulae and galaxies. When he came across Uranus, he thought that he had discovered a comet. However, after several months of observation, Anders Lexell, a mathematician, calculated its orbit and found that it was completely outside Saturn's orbit. It was a new planet! No one had expected to find more planets.

Many moons and more

The *Voyager 2* spacecraft flew by Uranus in 1986 and provided the first closeup images. The third largest gas giant has a faint ring system, over 20 moons and a simple cloud system. Uranus also rotates on its side, like a rolling ball, because its axis is titled 98° from vertical.

Uranus' pale blue color comes from a small amount of methane in its atmosphere. Like the other gas giants, its atmosphere is composed mainly of hydrogen gas, aurorae occur at its poles and lightning flashes within its atmosphere. The temperature at its cloudtops is −373° F.

Soup and Cyclops

Below its atmosphere at a depth of 3,000 to 4,000 miles lies something that scientists call "ice," but it is actually a hot, liquid soup of water, methane and ammonia. This ice extends all the way to a tiny rock core at the center of the planet.

Uranus was named after one of the earliest supreme gods in Greek mythology, who was the father of the Cyclops. William Herschel had proposed that his new planet be named after King George III of England, but the international consensus was to keep the names of the planets based in mythology.

Observing Uranus

Uranus is just visible to the naked eye but you have to know exactly where to look to find it because it blends in with all the other fainter stars. In a small telescope, Uranus appears as a pale blue dot with 100x magnification.

The size of the Sun from Uranus. Compare it to the others.

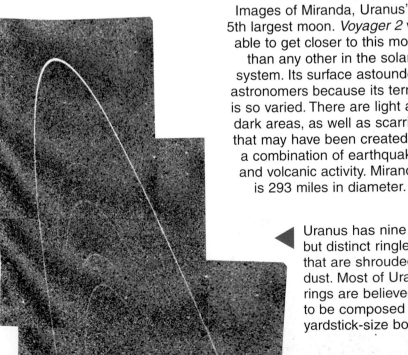

Images of Miranda, Uranus' 5th largest moon. *Voyager 2* was able to get closer to this moon than any other in the solar system. Its surface astounded astronomers because its terrain is so varied. There are light and dark areas, as well as scarring that may have been created by a combination of earthquake and volcanic activity. Miranda is 293 miles in diameter.

Uranus has nine faint but distinct ringlets that are shrouded in dust. Most of Uranus' rings are believed to be composed of yardstick-size boulders.

Neptune

Uranus was discovered accidentally; however, Neptune was discovered by mathematically calculating its position.

In the years following the discovery of Uranus, astronomers noticed that Uranus' path in the sky did not match the path computed by scientists. Uranus was straying from its computed course, but why? Some scientists thought the cause could be the gravitational attraction of an undiscovered planet.

In 1841, John Couch Adams of England calculated where this new planet might be found. But Adams did not engage in observational astronomy, so his results were forwarded to the Royal Observatory in Greenwich, England. Unfortunately, the director did not use this information to look for a possible new planet.

Four years later and independent of Adams, Urbain Le Verrier of France made his own calculations. He then asked Johann Galle, a German astronomer, to search for the planet. Galle found the planet the first night that he looked for it on September 23, 1846.

Neptune thus became the first of two planets discovered by using a scientific method of investigation. The other planet was Pluto. Neptune was named after the Roman god of the sea.

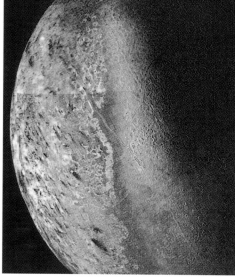

Triton, Neptune's largest moon. Although Triton was discovered just 17 days after Neptune, it was not named until 60 years later. As can be seen in this photograph, part of its surface resembles the skin of a cantaloupe. Triton has a thin atmosphere, ices on its surface and gaseous eruptions from its interior.

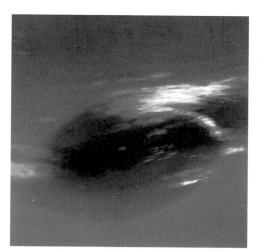

A closeup of the Great Dark Spot on Neptune. It is similar to the Great Red Spot on Jupiter and is a whirling vortex of clouds, like a hurricane. The whitish clouds near the top of the dark spot are compose of methane-ice.

Twin planets

Neptune is the smallest of the four gas giants but could be Uranus' twin because their diameters, colors, atmospheres and internal makeup are similar. Uranus and Neptune are the two most similar planets in our solar system.

Voyager 2's last call

In 1989, twelve years after it was launched from Earth, *Voyager 2* flew by Neptune. No one had ever seen this planet close up before.

Neptune is colder than Uranus because it is farther away from the Sun. This fact led scientists to believe that the atmosphere on Neptune would be much simpler and even plainer than on Uranus. But astronomers were surprised to find that Neptune's atmosphere is much more complex and beautiful than its twin. *Voyager 2* brought surprise after surprise on its journey through our solar system, and Neptune was the last planet that *Voyager* visited.

Observing Neptune

Neptune can be seen with binoculars or a small telescope, but like Uranus, you have to know exactly where to look because it blends in with the other fainter stars. You can just discern a hint of its blue-green disk in a telescope at 200x magnification.

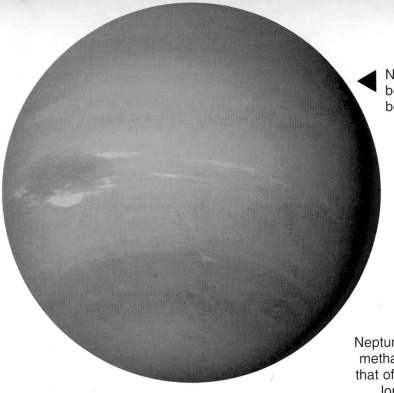

Neptune is the smallest of the four gas giants. This beautiful blue-green planet surprised astronomers because they expected it to look as plain as Uranus.

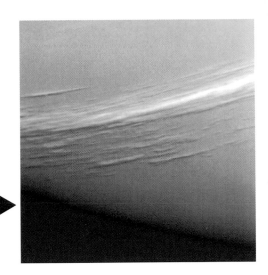

Neptune has whitish methane-ice clouds that often appear as long, thin wisps.

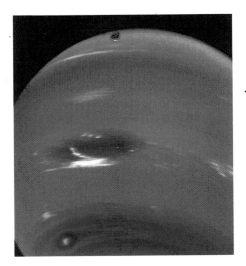

The Great Dark Spot of Neptune is not a permanent storm because no trace of it could be found on images taken by the *Hubble Space Telescope* in the late 1990s. At the bottom edge of this picture, just left of center, is an eye-like oval called the Small Dark Spot.

The size of the Sun from Neptune. Compare it to the others.

Two images of Neptune's rings taken 90 minutes apart by *Voyager 2*. The rings are faint and have what are called ring arcs. These ring arcs are short sections that appear brighter and thicker because ice and rock particles concentrate in these areas. The ring arcs cannot be seen in these pictures.

Neptune Facts

Diameter: 30,777 miles

Distance from the Sun: 2,794,000,000 miles

Outer atmosphere: 74% hydrogen, 25% helium, 1% methane

Inner core: possible small rock core surrounded by a soup of various "ices"

Temperature near cloudtops: −373° F

Rotation on Axis (Neptune's Day): 19 hours, 12 minutes

Revolution about Sun (Neptune's Year): 164 years

Moons: Neptune has 8 known moons. Triton, the largest, has a diameter of 1,678 miles and orbits Neptune in 5 days, 22 hours at a distance of 220,000 miles.

Pluto

On February 18, 1930, Clyde Tombaugh (pronounced TOM-bah) discovered Pluto from observations he made at the Lowell Observatory in Flagstaff, Arizona. For over 11 months, he searched for the ninth planet by carefully taking and examining photographs of the night sky. Pluto thus became the second planet that was discovered by using a scientific method of investigation.

How do you tell a planet from a star?

All the stars that we see in the sky are beyond our solar system and are so far away that they do not appear to move, not even in thousands of years. However, the planets do not stay in place but move among the fixed stars. The planets move because they are close to us and revolve around the Sun just like the Earth. The original meaning of the word planet is "wandering star." The ancients studied the sky and named five stars that did not stay in place. They called them Mercury, Venus, Mars, Jupiter and Saturn. Clyde Tombaugh used the idea that planets move against the background of stars to find Pluto.

Clyde Tombaugh's search

Tombaugh took hundreds of photographs to find Pluto using a special 13-inch diameter refractor telescope called an astrograph. Each photograph covered only a small area of the sky. Tombaugh also took his photographs near a path in the sky called the ecliptic. All of the planets, including the Sun and Moon can be found near this path because they all orbit the Sun in nearly the same plane. He reasoned that if there were a ninth planet,

it would also be near the ecliptic. Tombaugh took two photographs of the same area of the sky one week apart. He then compared these in a special optical instrument called a blinking comparator. This instrument allowed him to look back and forth between the two photographs. When the two photographs were aligned properly in the blinking comparator, the stars would not appear to move as the instrument quickly switched the view between the photographs. However, any object that moved during the one week period would appear to jump back and forth. This is how Tombaugh found Pluto. It appeared as a very faint dot jumping back and forth between two photographs in the blinking comparator.

The naming of the ninth planet

The Lowell Observatory asked the public for help in naming the ninth planet. People from all over the world mailed in their suggestions. Pluto, the Roman god of the underworld, was chosen from a submission sent in by Venetia Burney, an 11 year old girl from Oxford, England.

Pluto is a planet!

A few astronomers have suggested that Pluto should not be called a planet but should be considered a large outer comet-type object. Most astronomers do not agree and consider Pluto a planet!

Exploring Pluto

Pluto is the only planet that has not been visited by a spacecraft. In the near future, scientists are hoping to launch a spacecraft that will go to our most distant planet. The journey to Pluto is expected to take from 6 to 14 or more years depending on when the spacecraft is launched.

Pluto Facts

Diameter: 1,429 miles

Distance from the Sun: 3,675,000,000 miles

Atmosphere: Maybe 100% methane? Some helium?

Composition: Pluto may be composed of frozen ices and rock-type material. Two of the ices may be frozen water and nitrogen.

Temperature: −419° F

Rotation on Axis (Pluto's Day): 6 days, 10 hours

Revolution about Sun (Pluto's Year): 248 years

Moon: Pluto has one moon named Charon which is 746 miles in diameter and orbits Pluto in 6 days, 10 hours at a distance of 11,900 miles.

This is the best image of Pluto and represents a composite of many images taken by the *Hubble Space Telescope* that orbits Earth. The surface of Pluto has lighter and darker regions that may represent icy and rocky areas.

The size of the Sun from Pluto. Compare it to the others.

Pluto and its moon Charon as imaged by the *Hubble Space Telescope*.

Orbits of inner planets —
Mercury, Venus, Earth and Mars

Jupiter's Orbit
Saturn's Orbit
Uranus' Orbit
Neptune's Orbit

Pluto's Orbit

Pluto's orbit is highly inclined to the rest of the planets and part of it, the red segment, lies inside Neptune's orbit.

30

Comets

Comets are the most spectacular objects that can grace our night skies. They are members of our solar system just like the planets and asteroids. Comets have been observed throughout history and appear frequently enough that most of us will see at least one during our lives. Comets are named after those who discover them.

Dirty snowballs

Comets are material left over from the formation of the solar system 4.5 billion years ago. They are often referred to as dirty snowballs because they are composed of a mixture of ices and sand particles. The ices are water ice as well as frozen chemicals like carbon dioxide, which is also known as "dry ice."

Across the solar system

Unlike the planets, the orbits of comets are very elongated. One end often comes close to the Sun while the other end is often beyond Pluto.

When comets are farther away than Jupiter, their cores or nuclei remain frozen balls of ices and rock particles. As they get closer to the Sun, at about the distance of Jupiter's orbit, the ices in the nucleus start to turn to gas, releasing sand particles. This creates a halo around the nucleus, called the coma, and a tail that extends outward. As the comet gets even closer to the Sun, more and more of the ices change to gas, creating a larger and brighter coma and a longer tail. The tail can stretch across the night sky, extending for a hundred million miles or more through the solar system. The tail always points away from the Sun. Sometimes, two tails form.

◄ Comet Hale-Bopp was one of the most beautiful comets to grace our skies at the end of the 20th century. This comet had two tails, a blue one that was created by fluorescing ions and a whitish dust tail. Hale-Bopp was considered a large comet. Its nucleus was about 37 miles in diameter and its tails stretched for nearly 140 million miles. Hale-Bopp will return in the year 4390.

Three belts of comets

Astronomers believe there are three belts of comets. The outermost belt is called the Oort cloud. The comets in this group have orbits that extend much farther than Pluto and possibly halfway to the star closest to the Sun, Proxima Centauri. These comets take tens of thousands of years to orbit the Sun and number in the billions.

The second group resides in what is called the Kuiper belt. These comets have orbits whose farthest ends can be as close as Neptune or stretch out beyond Pluto. Comet Halley is in this belt.

Comets in the innermost belt circle the Sun in orbits that stretch no farther than Jupiter. This small group of comets was roped in by the strong gravitational pull of Jupiter. When the more distant comets from the Kuiper belt and Oort cloud come close to the Sun, they can be pulled in to shorter orbits if they come close to Jupiter's huge gravitational pull.

Famous comets

Halley's Comet. The most famous of all comets. Comet Halley regularly returns to the inner part of the solar system every 76 years. Edmund Halley (pronounced HAL-lee) was not the first person to see this comet but was the first person to recognize it as the same comet that had appeared at least twice before. Halley's comet will make its next appearance around 2062.

Comet Shoemaker-Levy 9's collision with Jupiter. In 1994, comet Shoemaker-Levy 9 collided with Jupiter. Most life on Earth would have been destroyed if it had hit the Earth. Astronomers believe that Jupiter may act like a helpful magnet by gravitationally sucking in comets that would otherwise hit Earth.

Comet Hale-Bopp. One of the biggest and brightest comets of the 20th century. Thomas Bopp discovered this comet while looking through a telescope near Phoenix, Arizona, and Alan Hale saw it 15 minutes later from New Mexico. Hale reported the discovery before Bopp.

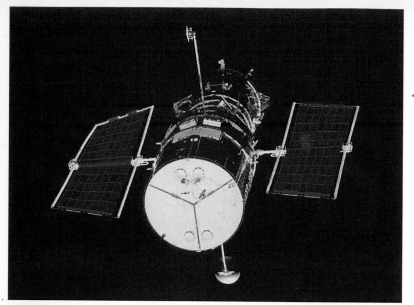

The *Hubble Space Telescope* has revolutionized our understanding of the universe. The two solar panels on opposite sides provide power.

Telescope stores offer a variety of telescopes and accessories.

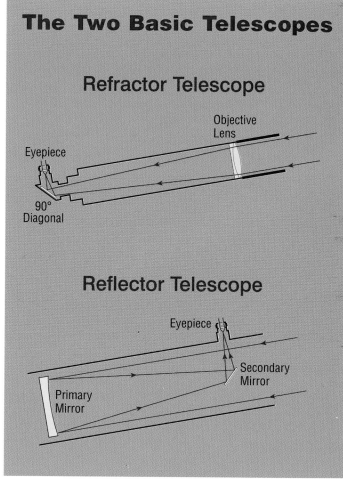

The Two Basic Telescopes

Refractor Telescope

Objective Lens

Eyepiece

90° Diagonal

Reflector Telescope

Eyepiece

Secondary Mirror

Primary Mirror

The *Gemini North* reflector telescope that sits atop Mauna Kea in Hawaii.

Right. Inside the dome. The mirror of the *Gemini North* telescope has a diameter of 26 feet.

Far right. The dome at sunset.

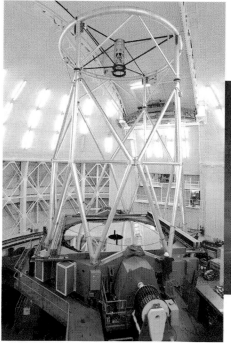

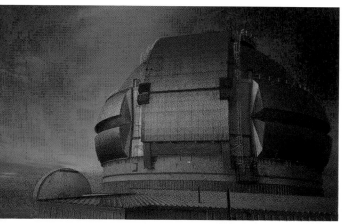

Telescopes

Astronomers use telescopes to study the heavens. The first telescope was invented 400 years ago and helped provide the evidence that the Earth was not the center of all creation, just a planet orbiting a star.

Refractors & reflectors

The two basic types of telescope are the refractor and reflector. The refractor was invented by the Dutch scientist Hans Lippershey in 1608. Just one year later in 1609, Galileo Galilei of Italy made several small refractors (all less than two inches in diameter) and became one of the first scientists to explore and make drawings of what he saw in the sky. In 1668, Sir Isaac Newton of England made the first reflecting telescope with a mirror diameter of a few inches. By 1800, reflecting telescopes with diameters of 48 inches were in use.

The largest telescopes

The 40-inch diameter Yerkes telescope located in Williams Bay, Wisconsin, is the largest refractor in the world. It was completed in 1897 and named after Charles Yerkes, a rich transportation tycoon who provided the money to build it. Large refractors are no longer made because they are more costly and not as practical as reflecting telescopes.

One of the largest telescopes in the world is the *Gemini North* telescope that sits atop the 13,800 foot high Mauna Kea mountain in Hawaii. This reflector telescope has a mirror diameter of 26 feet. Like most modern professional telescopes, it will be shared by astronomers from all over the world to conduct research.

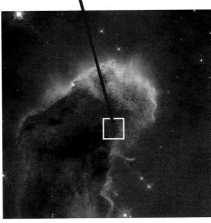

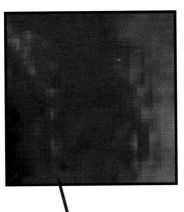

All spacecraft and most telescopes record images using digital technology, similar to that used in digital cameras. This picture was taken by the *Hubble Space Telescope* and is composed of thousands of squares or pixels, each containing information for just one color.

Our atmosphere and telescopes

The Earth's atmosphere limits the ability of telescopes to see fine detail. Although our atmosphere may seem clear and steady, it is constantly in motion with cooler and warmer pockets of air moving about. The future of astronomy lies with telescopes in space.

The *Hubble Space Telescope*

In 1990, the *Hubble Space Telescope* became the first optical telescope to be placed into orbit around Earth. With a mirror diameter of 94 inches (7 feet, 10 inches), its 375 mile high orbit puts it far above the atmosphere, allowing it to see more detail than any Earth-based telescope. The *Hubble Space Telescope* has revolutionized astronomy by providing the most spectacular and detailed images of heavenly bodies ever seen. In the future, the planned *Next Generation Telescope* will not orbit the Earth, but will instead be placed into orbit about the Sun, sharing Earth's orbit and staying at a fixed distance from us.

Digital images

The pictures obtained from the *Hubble Space Telescope*, as well as those from spacecraft, are digital pictures that use the same technology as digital cameras. Digital pictures are composed of many pixels or small squares. A pixel contains information for just one color, and this color information is easy to send over radio waves.

Most planetary pictures are composites. They are assembled from many smaller pictures taken by the digital cameras aboard spacecraft or used with telescopes. The picture of Mercury on page 9 is an obvious example of a composite.

Glossary

Ammonia. A strong smelling, colorless gas with molecules composed of one nitrogen and three hydrogen atoms. It is very soluble with water; that is, it can easily be mixed with water. Ammonia is not the same as pneumonia, which is an infection of the lungs.

Astronomer. A scientist who studies objects beyond Earth's atmosphere.

Atom. The smallest fundamental unit of matter. There are over 100 different atoms. The simplest and most abundant is hydrogen.

Aurora Borealis and Aurora Australis. Often called the Northern or Southern Lights. They are displays of illumination in the night sky caused by charged particles, blown off from the Sun, interacting with our atmosphere. The aurorae occur most often around the north and south poles where the Earth's magnetic field is concentrated. They appear as large patches in the sky, often shimmering, and can be red and green.

Compound. A substance that is created when two or more different atoms bond together. Atoms combine to form the different types of materials on Earth and in the universe. There are two main groups of compounds: inorganic and organic. Organic compounds contain carbon and are the building blocks of life.

Electron. Part of an atom. Electrons spin around the nucleus or center of atoms. The hydrogen atom has one electron. An iron atom has 26 electrons.

Element. A substance that cannot be further broken down into other substances. An element is composed of one type of atom. Hydrogen, iron, sulfur, aluminum and gold are elements.

Energy. An abstract concept that relates to ability to produce power. Light has energy to power a calculator or warm an atmosphere. Gasoline has energy to power cars.

F or Fahrenheit Temperature. The Fahrenheit temperature scale uses 0° F as the lowest temperature that can be achieved for a mixture of water, ice and salt before it freezes; and 212° F for the boiling point of pure water. The United States is one of the few remaining countries that still uses the Fahrenheit scale. Most of the world uses the Celsius temperature scale where pure water freezes at 0° and boils at 100°.

Galaxy. A grouping of billions of stars that often resembles a spiral. Galaxies are the homes of stars and are the largest structures in the universe.

Gas Giants. The planets Jupiter, Saturn, Uranus and Neptune. These planets are much larger than Earth and are composed mostly of hydrogen gas. They do not have a surface that you could stand on.

Gas. One of the three basic states of matter. Gas is the state where molecules move around the most freely. An example of a gaseous state is our atmosphere on Earth. The three basic states of matter are solid, liquid and gas.

Greeks. The ancients Greeks created an intellectual and democratic culture that flourished from 800 to 200 B.C. in and around Greece. Socrates, Plato and Aristotle were famous Greek philosophers. The religion of the ancient Greeks, which is known today as Greek mythology, was based on multiple gods.

Helium. The second most abundant element or atom in the universe. Helium is formed in the center of stars.

Hydrogen. The most abundant element or atom in the universe. Hydrogen is a gas on Earth, but in the cores of the larger planets, it is compressed into a solid and acts like a metal. Stars are made mostly of hydrogen.

Image. A likeness of an object or scene that is brought to focus by a telescope or camera lens. Images are often recorded on photo-

Glossary

graphic film or light sensitive electronic chips such as those used in digital cameras. In everyday life, the word *image* is often used to refer to the reproduction of an object or scene. A photograph captures the images of people. A sculpture is the image of someone.

Ion. An atom or compound that has a positive or negative charge because it has lost or gained electrons. Ions can fluoresce, that is, they can give off their own light.

Iron. An element that is classified as a metal, and is the main substance of steel. Metals conduct electricity. Iron also has magnetic properties.

Light-year. A unit of distance that is based on the distance that light travels in one year. Light travels at a rate of 186,282 miles per second, so one light year is about six trillion miles.

Metal. A special class of material that is made of atoms which can conduct electricity. A few metals are aluminum, lead, steel, copper and iron. Steel is a metal made of several elements.

Methane. A colorless, odorless, flammable gas with molecules composed of one carbon and four hydrogen atoms. Methane is present on Earth and in the gas giants.

Molecule. The smallest particle that an element or compound can be divided into. Molecules of elements are single atoms. Molecules of compounds are several atoms that are joined or bonded together.

Mythology. The legends and myths of ancient civilizations. These legends and myths were the beliefs and religions of ancient cultures.

Nebula (plural is Nebulae). A giant hydrogen cloud in space where stars and solar systems are often born. The Orion Nebula is one of the best known nebulae.

Nickel. A metal element that is found on many rock-type planets and asteroids, including the Earth and our Moon. The coin that we call a nickel is partially made of this metal.

Northern Lights. *See* Aurora Borealis and Aurora Australis.

Photograph. The recording of an image of an object or scene digitally or on photographic film. Images are formed by a telescope or camera lens. They are then focused onto photographic film or a light sensitive electronic chip made up of thousands of tiny squares called pixels.

Picture. A representation of an actual object or scene created by drawing, painting, photography or other means.

Romans. The Roman empire, seated in Italy, existed from 753 B.C. to 450 A.D. They adopted many mythological religious beliefs from the Greeks, whom they conquored in 170 B.C.

Sand. Small rock particles. Rocks are a mixture of various compounds.

Scientist. A person who examines and studies the world around us using standardized methods of investigation.

Terrestrial Planets. Mercury, Venus, Earth and Mars. These planets are rock-like and have a surface that you can stand on. Pluto is not considered a terrestrial planet because ices may be a large part of its makeup.

Universe. Everything. The space where all the galaxies reside. When you look up at the night sky, you are looking at a part of the universe.

Voyager 1 & 2. Two of the most successful spacecraft that explored the outer planets of our solar system. *Voyager 1* visited Jupiter and Saturn while *Voyager 2* visited these two planets as well as Uranus and Neptune. These two spacecraft are often referred to by the name *Voyager*.

Contributors

Ken Graun is the author of the popular astronomy field guide, *What's Out Tonight? 50 Year Astronomy Field Guide, 2000 to 2050.* He also coauthored, with David Levy, the beginner's star chart, *David H. Levy's Guide to the Stars.* Ken lectures and is writing more astronomy books for beginners and children.

Thomas J. Bopp codiscovered the spectacular Comet Hale-Bopp. He lectures and shares astronomy with others.

Debra K. Niwa is an experienced art director who has designed the covers and layouts for numerous magazines and books.

From left: Ken Graun, Debra K. Niwa and Thomas J. Bopp

Special thanks to Marie McFarland for proofreading, Julianne Hurst-Williams for photography, David & Wendee Levy for support and Suzanne Graun for her understanding.

Website Support

Our website has specific information to help readers conduct the **Try This** sections featured in this book. And, there is additional information on the website so readers can learn more about astronomy.

VISIT

whatsouttonight.com

Photo Credits

Front covers. Sun: NASA/ESA, Mercury: NASA, Venus: NASA/ARC, Earth: NASA, Mars: AURA/NASA/ESA, Jupiter-Saturn-Uranus-Neptune: JPL, Pluto: NASA/ESA. *Back covers.* Earth: NASA. *Inside front dust cover.* JPL. *Inside back dust cover.* JULIANNE HURST-WILLIAMS. *Front end pages.* Sun: NASA/ESA, Mercury: NASA, Venus: NASA/ARC, Earth: NASA, Mars: AURA/NASA/ESA, Jupiter-Saturn-Uranus-Neptune: JPL, Pluto: NASA/ESA. *Back end pages.* NASA/JPL. *Page 1.* NASA. *Page 3.* JULIANNE HURST-WILLIAMS. *Page 4/5.* Background: DEBRA K. NIWA. *Page 5 nebula:* JEFF HESTER AND PAUL SCOWEN (ARIZONA STATE UNIVERSITY) AND NASA. *Page 6.* Sun: NASA/ESA, Eclipse: AURA/NOAO/NSF, Prominence: AURA/NOAO/NSF. *Page 7.* AURA/NOAO/NSF. *Page 8.* Top: NASA, Bottom: NORTHWESTERN UNIVERSITY. *Page 9.* NASA. *Page 10.* Top: JPL, Pioneer Venus: NASA/JPL, Bottom left: NASA/ARC, Bottom right: JPL. *Page 12/13.* Earth: JPL, All others: NASA. *Page 14/15.* Moon: UCO/Lick Observatory, All others: NASA. *Page 16/17.* Mars top left: MALIN SPACE SCIENCE SYSTEMS, Olympus Mons-Phobes-Demios-South polar cap: JPL, Mars by Hubble Space Telescope: AURA/NASA/ESA, Bottom panorama: JPL. *Page 18/19.* Background: DEBRA K. NIWA, Kleopatra: ARECIBO OBSERVATORY, Ida: JPL. *Page 20.* Top four pictures: JPL, Io: US GEOLOGICAL SURVEY, Europe: GALILEO PROJECT/UNIVERSITY OF ARIZONA/JPL/NASA. *Page 21.* DLR. *Page 22–27.* JPL. *Page 29.* Top: NASA/ESA, Middle: A. STERN (SWRI)/M. BUIE (LOWELL OBS.)/NASA/ESA. *Page 31.* BILL AND SALLY FLETCHER. *Page 32.* Hubble Space Telescope: NASA, Telescope store: DEAN KOENIG/STARIZONA/TUCSON, ARIZONA, Gemini North: AURA/NOAO/NSF. *Page 31.* JEFF HESTER AND PAUL SCOWEN (ARIZONA STATE UNIVERSITY) AND NASA.

How much would you weigh on...

Find Your Earth Weight →

	Mercury	Venus	Moon	Mars	Pluto
45 pounds	17 lbs	40 lbs	8 lbs	17 lbs	4 lbs
50 pounds	19 lbs	45 lbs	8 lbs	19 lbs	4 lbs
55 pounds	21 lbs	50 lbs	9 lbs	21 lbs	4 lbs
60 pounds	23 lbs	54 lbs	10 lbs	23 lbs	5 lbs
65 pounds	25 lbs	58 lbs	11 lbs	25 lbs	5 lbs
70 pounds	27 lbs	63 lbs	12 lbs	27 lbs	6 lbs
75 pounds	28 lbs	68 lbs	13 lbs	28 lbs	6 lbs
80 pounds	30 lbs	72 lbs	14 lbs	30 lbs	6 lbs
85 pounds	32 lbs	76 lbs	14 lbs	32 lbs	7 lbs
90 pounds	34 lbs	81 lbs	15 lbs	34 lbs	7 lbs
95 pounds	36 lbs	86 lbs	16 lbs	36 lbs	8 lbs
100 pounds	38 lbs	90 lbs	17 lbs	38 lbs	8 lbs

What about Jupiter, Saturn, Uranus and Neptune? These planets are giant balls of gas and do not have a surface that you can stand on. They could only be visited by staying in a spacecraft that orbited the planet. Normally you are weightless in a spacecraft that orbits a planet.

The amount of time it would take to travel from the Sun to...

	At 75 Miles per Hour	At the Speed of Light ✢
Mercury	55 years	3.2 minutes
Venus	102 years	6 minutes
Earth✢✢	142 years	8.3 minutes
Mars	216 years	12.7 minutes
Asteroid Belt	266 to 571 years	16 to 34 minutes
Jupiter	736 years	43 minutes
Saturn	1,350 years	1 hour, 19 minutes
Uranus	2,715 years	2 hours, 40 minutes
Neptune	4,253 years	4 hours, 10 minutes
Pluto	5,594 years	5 hours, 30 minutes
Nearest Star✢✢✢	38 million years	4 years, 3 months

✢ The speed of light is 186,282 miles per second.

✢✢ It would take 130 days to travel from the Earth to the Moon at 75 miles per hour or 1.3 seconds at the speed of light.

✢✢✢ The nearest star is called Proxima Centauri and is in the constellation Centaurus, located in the southern hemisphere. This star is not visible to the naked eye.

I WAS BORN ABOUT 10,000 YEARS AGO

A TALL TALE RETOLD AND ILLUSTRATED BY
STEVEN KELLOGG

Morrow Junior Books
New York

Colored inks, watercolors, and acrylics were used for the full-color illustrations. The text type is 14-point Palatino.

Copyright © 1996 by Steven Kellogg

Printed in the United States of America.

1 2 3 4 5 6 7 8 9 10

Library of Congress Cataloging-in-Publication Data
Kellogg, Steven.
I was born about 10,000 years ago: a tall tale / retold and illustrated by Steven Kellogg.
p. cm.
Summary: Born about 100 centuries ago, the narrator has seen many things happen since he watched Adam and Eve eat an apple.
ISBN 0-688-13411-4 (trade)—ISBN 0-688-13412-2 (library)   [1. Tall tales.   2. Humorous stories.   3. Stories in rhyme.]
I. Title.   II. Title: I was born about ten thousand years ago. PZ8.3.K33Iam 1996 [E]—dc20 95-35079 CIP AC

For the two heroic Colins, with love

AUTHOR'S NOTE

In *Huckleberry Finn*, Mark Twain's greatest novel, the hero accuses his creator of having told "some stretchers." Telling stretchers—elasticizing the truth and peppering it with humor—was indeed standard practice in nineteenth-century American storytelling. Whenever yarn spinners gathered, a spirit of good-natured one-upmanship led to bouts of boasting and outrageous exaggeration that gave birth to many a tall tale. *I Was Born about 10,000 Years Ago,* in which the narrator boldly injects himself into various biblical and historical settings, with improbable and humorous results, springs from that period. The tall-tale spirit of a century ago continues, inviting all of us to unfetter our imaginations and let them soar.

I was born about ten thousand years ago,
And there's nothing in the world that I don't know.

I saw King Pharaoh's daughter
Fishing Moses from the water,

And I'll lick the guy who says it isn't so.

I saw Satan when he looked the garden o'er,

I saw Eve and Adam driven from the door,
And from the bushes peeping,
Saw the apple they'd been eating,

And I swear that I'm the one who ate the core.

I taught Samson how to use his mighty hands,

Showed Columbus how to reach this happy land,

And for Pharaoh's little kiddies
I built all the pyramiddies

And to Sahara carried all the sand.

Queen Elizabeth she fell in love with me,
We were married in Milwaukee secretly,

But when sneezing overtook her

I went off with General Hooker

A-shootin' skeeters down in Tennessee.

When attacked once by a raging dinosaur,

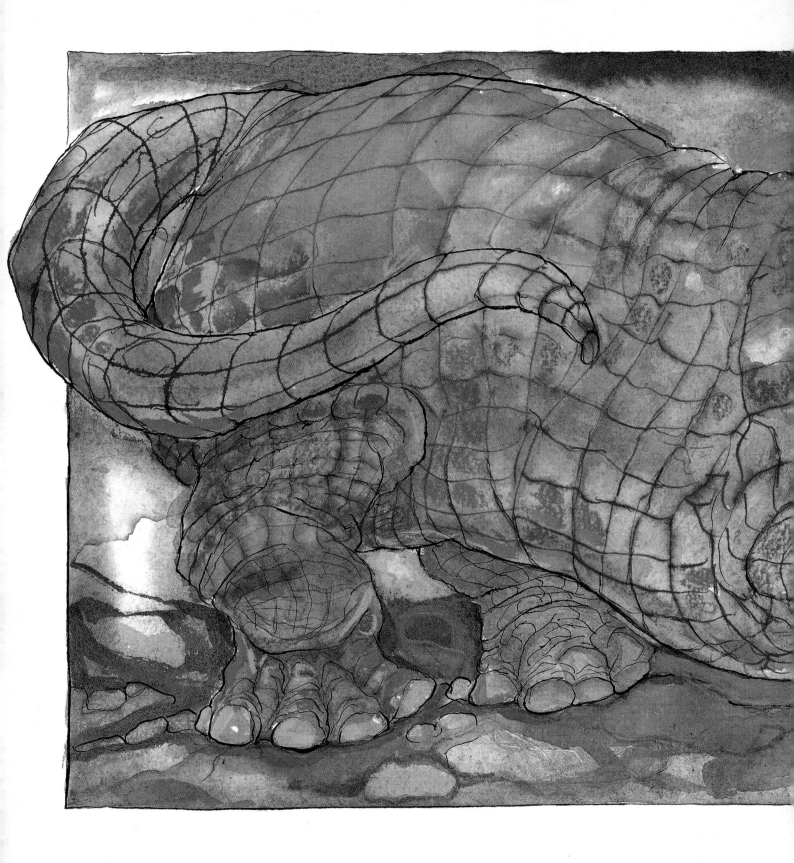

I said to him, "Why snarl and rant and roar?
You've been misunderstood.
Deep inside you're kind and good."

CHAPTER 9
THE
SEESAWRUS

CHAPTER 10
THE
CHAINSAWRUS

It was clear he'd never heard these words before.

When Paul Bunyan called for loggers I was there.

I helped Johnny plant each apple seed with care.

Pecos Bill and I drove cattle

Clear from Texas to Seattle,

Where I taught Mike Fink to wrestle grizzly bears.

I played hopscotch with some spacemen on the moon,

And I plan to visit Saturn very soon.

But first I'll need a rocket,
And a lot of food to stock it,

Since I won't be back till school gets out next June.

We've stretched the truth a bit, but now we're through.
The next tall tale will have to come from you.
Putting whoppers into rhyme
Was the way folks passed the time
For about a million years, or maybe two!

ACHOO

I WAS BORN ABOUT 10,000 YEARS AGO

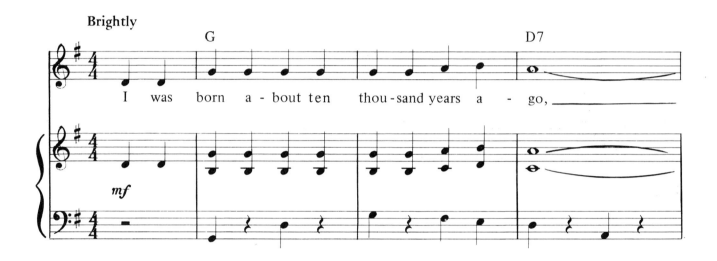

I was born a-bout ten thou-sand years a-go,

And there's noth-ing in the world that I don't know.